THE
BOOK
OF
hope

Tyndale House Publishers, Inc.
WHEATON, ILLINOIS

CONTENTS

Who Is God?

Thousands of years ago, Pharaoh, the ruler of Egypt, posed a question people are still asking today: "Who is the Lord that I should listen to him?" It is difficult for our limited mind to grasp the limitless, eternal God. It has been said, "If God were small enough for your mind, he wouldn't be big enough for your needs." For that reason, we shouldn't be exasperated if we cannot fully understand who God is or why he does certain things. One day, just as the apostle Paul assured the Corinthian church, everything about God and his character will be made perfectly clear to us. But until then, we will find everything we need to know about him in his Word.

God Is Our Creator

PSALM 139:1-24

For the choir director: A psalm of David.

¹O LORD, you have examined my heart and know everything about me. ²You know when I sit down or stand up. You know my every thought when far away. ³You chart the path ahead of me and tell me where to stop and rest. Every moment you know where I am. ⁴You know what I am going to say even before I say it, LORD. ⁵You both precede and follow me. You

1

place your hand of blessing on my head. ⁶Such knowledge is too wonderful for me, too great for me to know!

⁷I can never escape from your spirit! I can never get away from your presence! ⁸If I go up to heaven, you are there; if I go down to the place of the dead, you are there. ⁹If I ride the wings of the morning, if I dwell by the farthest oceans, ¹⁰even there your hand will guide me, and your strength will support me. ¹¹I could ask the darkness to hide me and the light around me to become night— ¹²but even in darkness I cannot hide from you. To you the night shines as bright as day. Darkness and light are both alike to you.

¹³You made all the delicate, inner parts of my body and knit me together in my mother's womb. ¹⁴Thank you for making me so wonderfully complex! Your workmanship is marvelous—and how well I know it. ¹⁵You watched me as I was being formed in utter seclusion, as I was woven together in the dark of the womb. ¹⁶You saw me before I was born. Every day of my life was recorded in your book. Every moment was laid out before a single day had passed.

¹⁷How precious are your thoughts about me, O God! They are innumerable! ¹⁸I can't even count them; they outnumber the grains of sand! And when I wake up in the morning, you are still with me!

¹⁹O God, if only you would destroy the wicked! Get out of my life, you murderers! ²⁰They blaspheme you; your enemies take your name in vain. ²¹O LORD, shouldn't I hate those who hate you? Shouldn't I despise those who resist you? ²²Yes, I hate them with complete hatred, for your enemies are my enemies.

²³Search me, O God, and know my heart; test me and know my thoughts. ²⁴Point out anything in me that offends you, and lead me along the path of everlasting life.

INSIGHTS FOR LIFE
Scripture teaches us about many of God's characteristics. This psalm highlights a few of them. God is our Creator, and he

knows every detail about what is going on in his amazing and
complex creation—including our life. But God does not simply
know about our life; he is intimately involved in it and always
present with us. As the psalmist says, there is no place we can go
to escape the presence of God. This brings comfort to those who
know that they need God's help but discomfort to those who wish
to hide from God. God's presence should motivate us to live a life
pleasing to him.

God Is Powerful and Personal

ACTS 17:22-30

²²So Paul, standing before the Council, addressed them as follows: "Men of Athens, I notice that you are very religious, ²³for as I was walking along I saw your many altars. And one of them had this inscription on it—'To an Unknown God.' You have been worshiping him without knowing who he is, and now I wish to tell you about him.

²⁴"He is the God who made the world and everything in it. Since he is Lord of heaven and earth, he doesn't live in man-made temples, ²⁵and human hands can't serve his needs—for he has no needs. He himself gives life and breath to everything, and he satisfies every need there is. ²⁶From one man he created all the nations throughout the whole earth. He decided beforehand which should rise and fall, and he determined their boundaries.

²⁷"His purpose in all of this was that the nations should seek after God and perhaps feel their way toward him and find him—though he is not far from any one of us. ²⁸For in him we live and move and exist. As one of your own poets says, 'We are his offspring.' ²⁹And since this is true, we shouldn't think of God as an idol designed by craftsmen from gold or silver or stone. ³⁰God overlooked people's former ignorance about these things, but now he commands everyone everywhere to turn away from idols and turn to him."

Paul's audience in this passage included people of two different beliefs. There were those who did not believe in life after death and who lived only for pleasure (the Epicureans). There were also those who believed that God existed in every material object and who sought to be at peace with the world around them (the Stoics). In speaking to these two groups, Paul showed them how their philosophies fell short of grasping the true nature of God. He did this by explaining first that God is the all-powerful Creator. Then he showed that God is not just an impersonal force but a being deeply concerned about maintaining intimate relationships with the people he created. We can be thankful that the true God not only created us but also sustains us, loves us, and desires an intimate relationship with us.

God Is Loving and Just

ROMANS 3:22-28

²²We are made right in God's sight when we trust in Jesus Christ to take away our sins. And we all can be saved in this same way, no matter who we are or what we have done.

²³For all have sinned; all fall short of God's glorious standard. ²⁴Yet now God in his gracious kindness declares us not guilty. He has done this through Christ Jesus, who has freed us by taking away our sins. ²⁵For God sent Jesus to take the punishment for our sins and to satisfy God's anger against us. We are made right with God when we believe that Jesus shed his blood, sacrificing his life for us. God was being entirely fair and just when he did not punish those who sinned in former times. ²⁶And he is entirely fair and just in this present time when he declares sinners to be right in his sight because they believe in Jesus.

²⁷Can we boast, then, that we have done anything to be accepted by God? No, because our acquittal is not based on our good deeds. It is based on our faith. ²⁸So we are made right with God through faith and not by obeying the law.

This passage shows two important and seemingly contradictory aspects of God's character: love and justice. The Bible tells us that God is loving. Despite God's knowledge of our sin, he reached out to offer us forgiveness through the death of his Son on the cross. But God's love is often misunderstood. Many think that because he loves us, he will overlook our sins. But the fact that God is loving does not negate the fact that he is also just. Scripture repeatedly makes the point that only the godly will see God's face. We can be certain that our sins must be dealt with, either by accepting God's gift of salvation through faith or by suffering God's ultimate judgment. The choice is ours to make, and God desires that all would receive his forgiveness.

Who Is Jesus?

Throughout history people have tried to answer this question. Our best source for finding an answer to this question is the Bible. Anyone who seriously studies Scripture to learn more about Jesus must answer two probing questions: What do you think of Jesus Christ? and Who is he? Writer C. S. Lewis made this observation in his book *Mere Christianity* (chapter 3): "You must make your choice. Either this man was and is the Son of God, or else he is a madman or something worse. You can shut him up for a fool, you can spit at him and kill him as a demon, or you can fall at his feet and call him Lord and God. But let us not come with any patronizing nonsense about his being a great human teacher. He has not left that open to us. He did not intend to." Jesus was not just a good man. He was—and is—the God-man.

Jesus Is Divine

COLOSSIANS 1:15-23

¹⁵Christ is the visible image of the invisible God. He existed before God made anything at all and is supreme over all creation. ¹⁶Christ is the one through whom God created everything in heaven and earth. He made the things we can see and the things we can't see—kings, kingdoms, rulers, and authorities. Everything has been created through him and for him.

[17]He existed before everything else began, and he holds all creation together.

[18]Christ is the head of the church, which is his body. He is the first of all who will rise from the dead, so he is first in everything. [19]For God in all his fullness was pleased to live in Christ, [20]and by him God reconciled everything to himself. He made peace with everything in heaven and on earth by means of his blood on the cross. [21]This includes you who were once so far away from God. You were his enemies, separated from him by your evil thoughts and actions, [22]yet now he has brought you back as his friends. He has done this through his death on the cross in his own human body. As a result, he has brought you into the very presence of God, and you are holy and blameless as you stand before him without a single fault. [23]But you must continue to believe this truth and stand in it firmly. Don't drift away from the assurance you received when you heard the Good News. The Good News has been preached all over the world, and I, Paul, have been appointed by God to proclaim it.

INSIGHTS FOR LIFE

The most crucial truth of the Christian faith is that Jesus Christ, though he came to earth as a man, was in fact God. Several statements in this passage point to the divinity of Jesus. He is eternal, existing even before the creation of the world. Jesus himself created this world and all things in it. Since creating the world, Jesus continues to sustain it and hold all things together. In the world, believers are led by Christ, the head of the church. Christ is also our leader regarding the resurrection, for he defeated death and paved the way for us to one day rise from the dead. Finally, Jesus, as both man and God, brought peace between his broken and sinful creation and our holy God.

Jesus Is Human

PHILIPPIANS 2:3-11

[3]Don't be selfish; don't live to make a good impression on others. Be humble, thinking of others as better than yourself.

⁴Don't think only about your own affairs, but be interested in others, too, and what they are doing.

⁵Your attitude should be the same that Christ Jesus had. ⁶Though he was God, he did not demand and cling to his rights as God. ⁷He made himself nothing; he took the humble position of a slave and appeared in human form. ⁸And in human form he obediently humbled himself even further by dying a criminal's death on a cross. ⁹Because of this, God raised him up to the heights of heaven and gave him a name that is above every other name, ¹⁰so that at the name of Jesus every knee will bow, in heaven and on earth and under the earth, ¹¹and every tongue will confess that Jesus Christ is Lord, to the glory of God the Father.

INSIGHTS FOR LIFE

Jesus became our supreme example as God in human form. He took the identity of a slave, refusing to cling to his privileges as God. Jesus—God in human form—experienced hunger. He endured sorrow. He grew tired. He felt the sting of loneliness. He felt the pressure of temptation. For these reasons, we can be assured that God understands what we are going through in life. But we can be thankful that Jesus was not just a man. He was able to rise above human circumstances to reconcile sinful people to a holy God. At the end of time, every knee will bow and every tongue will confess that Jesus Christ is Lord. Christ's divine nature, which he veiled at times during his earthly life, will then be clearly visible for all to see.

Jesus Made the Ultimate Sacrifice

ISAIAH 53:1-12

¹Who has believed our message? To whom will the LORD reveal his saving power? ²My servant grew up in the LORD's presence like a tender green shoot, sprouting from a root in dry and sterile ground. There was nothing beautiful or majestic about his appearance, nothing to attract us to him. ³He was despised

and rejected—a man of sorrows, acquainted with bitterest grief. We turned our backs on him and looked the other way when he went by. He was despised, and we did not care.

⁴Yet it was our weaknesses he carried; it was our sorrows that weighed him down. And we thought his troubles were a punishment from God for his own sins! ⁵But he was wounded and crushed for our sins. He was beaten that we might have peace. He was whipped, and we were healed! ⁶All of us have strayed away like sheep. We have left God's paths to follow our own. Yet the LORD laid on him the guilt and sins of us all.

⁷He was oppressed and treated harshly, yet he never said a word. He was led as a lamb to the slaughter. And as a sheep is silent before the shearers, he did not open his mouth. ⁸From prison and trial they led him away to his death. But who among the people realized that he was dying for their sins—that he was suffering their punishment? ⁹He had done no wrong, and he never deceived anyone. But he was buried like a criminal; he was put in a rich man's grave.

¹⁰But it was the LORD's good plan to crush him and fill him with grief. Yet when his life is made an offering for sin, he will have a multitude of children, many heirs. He will enjoy a long life, and the LORD's plan will prosper in his hands. ¹¹When he sees all that is accomplished by his anguish, he will be satisfied. And because of what he has experienced, my righteous servant will make it possible for many to be counted righteous, for he will bear all their sins. ¹²I will give him the honors of one who is mighty and great, because he exposed himself to death. He was counted among those who were sinners. He bore the sins of many and interceded for sinners.

INSIGHTS FOR LIFE
Death on the cross was not a rude interruption of the otherwise wonderful ministry of a great teacher. Jesus chose to take the punishment for our sins because he knew that there was no other way for us to approach a holy God. The fact that Jesus

knew what awaited him at the cross makes his journey to earth even more amazing. Christ's terrible death on the cross reveals the depth of our sin—it was a punishment that we deserved. It also demonstrates God's overwhelming love for us; our sin drove in the nails, but his love for us kept him on the cross. If there had been any other way for us to be forgiven, Jesus surely would have found it. But Jesus was willing to suffer this agonizing death for our salvation.

Jesus Defeated Satan for Us

1 JOHN 1:4-9

³We are telling you about what we ourselves have actually seen and heard, so that you may have fellowship with us. And our fellowship is with the Father and with his Son, Jesus Christ.

⁴We are writing these things so that our joy will be complete.

⁵This is the message he has given us to announce to you: God is light and there is no darkness in him at all. ⁶So we are lying if we say we have fellowship with God but go on living in spiritual darkness. We are not living in the truth. ⁷But if we are living in the light of God's presence, just as Christ is, then we have fellowship with each other, and the blood of Jesus, his Son, cleanses us from every sin.

⁸If we say we have no sin, we are only fooling ourselves and refusing to accept the truth. ⁹But if we confess our sins to him, he is faithful and just to forgive us and to cleanse us from every wrong.

INSIGHTS FOR LIFE
Though many people do not realize it, they are the target of a sinister plot. This plot is being carried out by Satan ("the Devil"), an angel who rebelled against God and who seeks to pervert and destroy God's good creation. The apostle Peter warns us, "Be careful! Watch out for attacks from the Devil, your great enemy. He prowls around like a roaring lion, looking for some victim to devour." But Jesus came to defeat Satan and

his schemes. Because of Jesus' death and resurrection, Satan's ultimate power over us is broken. We no longer need to sin because Christ gives us the power to live for him. We may still allow Satan to lead us astray from time to time, but ultimately we are not bound to follow him, for Christ is our new master.

Who Is the Holy Spirit?

The Holy Spirit is the most mysterious member of the Trinity, which includes God the Father, God the Son (Jesus Christ), and God the Holy Spirit. Many struggle with the idea of God's being three persons, yet one. Quite honestly, we will never fully grasp the concept this side of heaven. Some have wrongly thought of the Holy Spirit as an impersonal force rather than a person. Perhaps this comes from descriptions of his being like the wind or coming upon Jesus in the form of a dove. Yet these are simply metaphors used in Scripture to help communicate something of God's character. Similarly, Jesus described himself as "the Bread of Life" and "the Good Shepherd." Jesus said of the Holy Spirit: "When the Spirit of truth comes, he will guide you into all truth. . . . He will tell you about the future." Note the use of the pronoun *he*. The Holy Spirit has a distinct personality, and he has specific work that he wants to do in our life.

Why God Gives Us the Holy Spirit

EPHESIANS 1:9-14

⁹God's secret plan has now been revealed to us; it is a plan centered on Christ, designed long ago according to his good pleasure. ¹⁰And this is his plan: At the right time he will bring everything together under the authority of Christ—everything in heaven and on earth. ¹¹Furthermore, because of

Christ, we have received an inheritance from God, for he chose us from the beginning, and all things happen just as he decided long ago. ^{12}God's purpose was that we who were the first to trust in Christ should praise our glorious God. ^{13}And now you also have heard the truth, the Good News that God saves you. And when you believed in Christ, he identified you as his own by giving you the Holy Spirit, whom he promised long ago. ^{14}The Spirit is God's guarantee that he will give us everything he promised and that he has purchased us to be his own people. This is just one more reason for us to praise our glorious God.

INSIGHTS FOR LIFE
You might say that the Holy Spirit is our "identifying mark" as believers in Christ. In verses 13-14 we see three reasons why God gives us his Holy Spirit: First, God promised to send the Holy Spirit to those who trust Jesus Christ as Savior. The Holy Spirit also serves as a mark of ownership, showing that we belong to God. Lastly, the Holy Spirit represents God's guarantee or pledge to bring us to our final spiritual inheritance. This word translated "guarantee" could also be translated "first installment," signifying that this is just a small portion of what is awaiting us in heaven. God gives us the Holy Spirit not only to enable us to live out the Christian life but also to prove that we are precious in his sight.

How the Holy Spirit Works in Our Life
JOHN 14:12-21
^{12}"The truth is, anyone who believes in me will do the same works I have done, and even greater works, because I am going to be with the Father. ^{13}You can ask for anything in my name, and I will do it, because the work of the Son brings glory to the Father. ^{14}Yes, ask anything in my name, and I will do it!

^{15}"If you love me, obey my commandments. ^{16}And I will ask the Father, and he will give you another Counselor, who will never leave you. ^{17}He is the Holy Spirit, who leads into all truth. The world at large cannot receive him, because it isn't looking for him and doesn't recognize him. But you do, because he lives with you now and later will be in you. ¹⁸No, I will not abandon you as orphans—I will come to you. ¹⁹In just a little while the world will not see me again, but you will. For I will live again, and you will, too. ²⁰When I am raised to life again, you will know that I am in my Father, and you are in me, and I am in you. ²¹Those who obey my commandments are the ones who love me. And because they love me, my Father will love them, and I will love them. And I will reveal myself to each one of them."

INSIGHTS FOR LIFE

The New Testament describes three ways the Holy Spirit works in our life. Verse 17 shows two of these ways, and a third can be found elsewhere in Scripture. First, he works with us as non-believers. Before coming to belief in Jesus Christ, the Holy Spirit convicts us of our sin and reveals Christ as the answer. Second, he comes into our life when we turn to Christ. Once we accept Jesus Christ as our Savior and invite him into our life, the Holy Spirit moves into our life and sets up residence. Third, he empowers us as believers. This aspect of the Holy Spirit's work is described in Luke's Gospel, where Jesus says, "And now I will send the Holy Spirit, just as my Father promised."

Why We Need the Holy Spirit

GALATIANS 5:16-26

¹⁶So I advise you to live according to your new life in the Holy Spirit. Then you won't be doing what your sinful nature craves. ¹⁷The old sinful nature loves to do evil, which is just opposite from what the Holy Spirit wants. And the Spirit gives us desires that are opposite from what the sinful nature desires. These two forces are constantly fighting each other, and your choices are never free from this conflict. ¹⁸But when you are directed by the Holy Spirit, you are no longer subject to the law.

¹⁹When you follow the desires of your sinful nature, your lives will produce these evil results: sexual immorality, impure thoughts, eagerness for lustful pleasure, ²⁰idolatry, participation in demonic activities, hostility, quarreling, jealousy, outbursts of anger, selfish ambition, divisions, the feeling that everyone is wrong except those in your own little group, ²¹envy, drunkenness, wild parties, and other kinds of sin. Let me tell you again, as I have before, that anyone living that sort of life will not inherit the Kingdom of God.

²²But when the Holy Spirit controls our lives, he will produce this kind of fruit in us: love, joy, peace, patience, kindness, goodness, faithfulness, ²³gentleness, and self-control. Here there is no conflict with the law.

²⁴Those who belong to Christ Jesus have nailed the passions and desires of their sinful nature to his cross and crucified them there. ²⁵If we are living now by the Holy Spirit, let us follow the Holy Spirit's leading in every part of our lives. ²⁶Let us not become conceited, or irritate one another, or be jealous of one another.

INSIGHTS FOR LIFE

Living the Christian life is impossible without the Holy Spirit's help. This passage gives four reasons why we should relinquish control of our life to the Holy Spirit. First, he helps us make the right decisions if we listen to his advice. Second, he gives us the power to live by God's guidelines. Third, when we live by the Holy Spirit, he develops godly qualities—the fruit of the Spirit—in our life. Fourth, the Holy Spirit encourages us to seek God's approval above the approval of other people. In essence, the Holy Spirit enables Christians to live a life that is pleasing to God—something that is impossible to do on our own. He makes following Christ a joy rather than a duty.

The Hope of Heaven

Many people today believe that this present life is all there is—that when people die, they simply cease to exist forever. But this is not what the Bible teaches about life after death. The Bible makes it clear that there are great blessings in store for those who accept God's forgiveness for their sins and follow him. Such people will enter heaven, the perfect place where God reigns. We should also add that there is a place of punishment for those who do not follow God, and that place is called hell. Jesus often spoke of both destinies, and he called all people to turn from their sins and receive forgiveness so that they could one day enter heaven and live with him forever. More than a mere enticement to follow God, however, the promise of heaven gives God's people great hope—assurance that there is reward beyond this life so that we do not need to worry about the trials we must endure today.

What Is Heaven Like?

REVELATION 7:9-17

⁹After this I saw a vast crowd, too great to count, from every nation and tribe and people and language, standing in front of the throne and before the Lamb. They were clothed in white and held palm branches in their hands. ¹⁰And they

were shouting with a mighty shout, "Salvation comes from our God on the throne and from the Lamb!"

[11]And all the angels were standing around the throne and around the elders and the four living beings. And they fell face down before the throne and worshiped God. [12]They said,

"Amen! Blessing and glory and wisdom
and thanksgiving and honor and power and strength
belong to our God forever and forever. Amen!"

[13]Then one of the twenty-four elders asked me, "Who are these who are clothed in white? Where do they come from?"

[14]And I said to him, "Sir, you are the one who knows."

Then he said to me, "These are the ones coming out of the great tribulation. They washed their robes in the blood of the Lamb and made them white. [15]That is why they are standing in front of the throne of God, serving him day and night in his Temple. And he who sits on the throne will live among them and shelter them. [16]They will never again be hungry or thirsty, and they will be fully protected from the scorching noontime heat. [17]For the Lamb who stands in front of the throne will be their Shepherd. He will lead them to the springs of life-giving water. And God will wipe away all their tears."

INSIGHTS FOR LIFE

What will life in heaven be like? This passage in Revelation reveals several truths about the place where all believers will live forever. First, we will live without fear and worry. Heaven is a place of safety and protection. In heaven we will also live without need. Heaven is a place of complete sufficiency. Another wonderful truth is that we will live without pain. Heaven is a place of comfort. Finally, in heaven we will live without sorrow, for heaven is a place of boundless joy. In heaven we will be free of life's cares and filled with the joy of being in God's presence.

Who Will Enter Heaven?

JOHN 14:1-11

[1]"Don't be troubled. You trust God, now trust in me. [2]There are many rooms in my Father's home, and I am going to prepare a place for you. If this were not so, I would tell you plainly. [3]When everything is ready, I will come and get you, so that you will always be with me where I am. [4]And you know where I am going and how to get there."

[5]"No, we don't know, Lord," Thomas said. "We haven't any idea where you are going, so how can we know the way?"

[6]Jesus told him, "I am the way, the truth, and the life. No one can come to the Father except through me. [7]If you had known who I am, then you would have known who my Father is. From now on you know him and have seen him!"

[8]Philip said, "Lord, show us the Father and we will be satisfied."

[9]Jesus replied, "Philip, don't you even yet know who I am, even after all the time I have been with you? Anyone who has seen me has seen the Father! So why are you asking to see him? [10]Don't you believe that I am in the Father and the Father is in me? The words I say are not my own, but my Father who lives in me does his work through me. [11]Just believe that I am in the Father and the Father is in me. Or at least believe because of what you have seen me do."

INSIGHTS FOR LIFE

Hollywood often depicts the gates of heaven as the place where you "plead your case" for the right to enter. In this passage, Jesus clearly explains that the only ones who will enter heaven are those who have accepted him as the way, the truth, and the life— not those who have the best arguments or who have performed the most good deeds. Heaven is not a court but a prepared place for prepared people. Those who believe in Jesus Christ can rest assured that their reservation for heaven has been made. And when it comes to accommodations, we need not worry, for Jesus himself has promised to prepare a place for us.

Forgiveness

One of the great principles of the Christian life is forgiveness. Jesus modeled this principle for us when he hung on the cross and prayed for the very people who had put him there. His words were so powerful and unexpected that they brought about the conversion of one of the thieves hanging on a cross next to him. Because Jesus completely forgave us, he wants us to follow his example by forgiving others. We need to follow Paul's instructions to the Ephesians, "Be kind to each other, tenderhearted, forgiving one another, just as God through Christ has forgiven you. Follow God's example in everything you do, because you are his dear children."

God Desires to Forgive Us

PSALM 130:1-8

A song for the ascent to Jerusalem.

¹From the depths of despair, O LORD, I call for your help. ²Hear my cry, O Lord. Pay attention to my prayer.

³LORD, if you kept a record of our sins, who, O Lord, could ever survive? ⁴But you offer forgiveness, that we might learn to fear you.

⁵I am counting on the LORD; yes, I am counting on him. I have put my hope in his word. ⁶I long for the Lord more than

sentries long for the dawn, yes, more than sentries long for the dawn.

⁷O Israel, hope in the LORD; for with the LORD there is unfailing love and an overflowing supply of salvation. ⁸He himself will free Israel from every kind of sin.

INSIGHTS FOR LIFE

Sometimes people picture God as simply a great judge who declares people innocent or guilty according to their deeds. But the psalmist knew that in his moment of greatest despair, he could call upon God, who desired to forgive him and rescue him from his sins. God does judge us, but he will also forgive us if we repent and turn to him, for he sent his only Son, Jesus Christ, to remove the penalty for our sin. Jesus, who is God the Son, died on the cross in our place, taking the punishment that we deserve. Because of this, we, like the psalmist, can hope in the Lord, who possesses "unfailing love and an overflowing supply of salvation."

Forgiveness Should Have No Limits

MATTHEW 18:21-35

²¹Then Peter came to him and asked, "Lord, how often should I forgive someone who sins against me? Seven times?"

²²"No!" Jesus replied, "seventy times seven!

²³"For this reason, the Kingdom of Heaven can be compared to a king who decided to bring his accounts up to date with servants who had borrowed money from him. ²⁴In the process, one of his debtors was brought in who owed him millions of dollars. ²⁵He couldn't pay, so the king ordered that he, his wife, his children, and everything he had be sold to pay the debt. ²⁶But the man fell down before the king and begged him, 'Oh, sir, be patient with me, and I will pay it all.' ²⁷Then the king was filled with pity for him, and he released him and forgave his debt.

²⁸"But when the man left the king, he went to a fellow servant who owed him a few thousand dollars. He grabbed

him by the throat and demanded instant payment. ²⁹His fellow servant fell down before him and begged for a little more time. 'Be patient and I will pay it,' he pleaded. ³⁰But his creditor wouldn't wait. He had the man arrested and jailed until the debt could be paid in full.

³¹"When some of the other servants saw this, they were very upset. They went to the king and told him what had happened. ³²Then the king called in the man he had forgiven and said, 'You evil servant! I forgave you that tremendous debt because you pleaded with me. ³³Shouldn't you have mercy on your fellow servant, just as I had mercy on you?' ³⁴Then the angry king sent the man to prison until he had paid every penny.

³⁵"That's what my heavenly Father will do to you if you refuse to forgive your brothers and sisters in your heart."

INSIGHTS FOR LIFE

The religious leaders of Jesus' day taught that those who had been wronged were to forgive someone two or three times—at the most! In this passage, Peter wondered if forgiving someone seven times would be enough from Jesus' perspective. Imagine Peter's shock when Jesus told him that he should forgive up to "seventy times seven"—490 times. Does this mean that we should deny forgiveness on the 491st offense? Of course not. Rather, Jesus was teaching that we should extend unlimited forgiveness to others. We, as sinners, have been forgiven much. So we ought to forgive those who have hurt us, no matter how badly. They owe us little compared to what we once owed God.

Forgiveness Is Not Selective

MATTHEW 5:38-48

³⁸"You have heard that the law of Moses says, 'If an eye is injured, injure the eye of the person who did it. If a tooth gets knocked out, knock out the tooth of the person who did it.' ³⁹But I say, don't resist an evil person! If you are slapped on

the right cheek, turn the other, too. [40]If you are ordered to court and your shirt is taken from you, give your coat, too. [41]If a soldier demands that you carry his gear for a mile, carry it two miles. [42]Give to those who ask, and don't turn away from those who want to borrow.

[43]"You have heard that the law of Moses says, 'Love your neighbor' and hate your enemy. [44]But I say, love your enemies! Pray for those who persecute you! [45]In that way, you will be acting as true children of your Father in heaven. For he gives his sunlight to both the evil and the good, and he sends rain on the just and on the unjust, too. [46]If you love only those who love you, what good is that? Even corrupt tax collectors do that much. [47]If you are kind only to your friends, how are you different from anyone else? Even pagans do that. [48]But you are to be perfect, even as your Father in heaven is perfect."

INSIGHTS FOR LIFE

It has been said, "To return evil for good is devilish; to return good for good is human. To return good for evil is divine." Although we are not divine, we, as believers, do not have the liberty to choose whom we will forgive or not forgive. We must do as Jesus has commanded and not only forgive our enemies but love them as well. Loving our enemies does not come easily, but it is what Jesus calls us to do. It was Jesus himself who gave us the ultimate example of what it means to forgive our enemies. While hanging on the cross, he prayed, "Father, forgive these people, because they don't know what they are doing." God's Spirit enables us to love, pray, and do good to those who hate us.

Love

On one occasion Jesus was asked what commandment was the most important. He replied, "The most important commandment is this: 'Hear, O Israel! The Lord our God is the one and only Lord. And you must love the Lord your God with all your heart, all your soul, all your mind, and all your strength.' The second is equally important: 'Love your neighbor as yourself.'" If we truly love God with all our heart, soul, mind, and strength, we will want to follow all his other commands. In the same way, if we really love others as much as we love ourselves, we will be concerned for their welfare and treat them accordingly. But before we can effectively love God, we must first realize how much he loves us. The apostle Paul explains that God showed his great love for us by sending Christ to die for us while we were still sinners. The more we realize this wonderful truth, the more our love for God will grow.

God Should Be the Greatest Love of Our Life
DEUTERONOMY 6:1-9

¹"These are all the commands, laws, and regulations that the LORD your God told me to teach you so you may obey them in the land you are about to enter and occupy, ²and so you and your children and grandchildren might fear the LORD your

God as long as you live. If you obey all his laws and commands, you will enjoy a long life. ³Listen closely, Israel, to everything I say. Be careful to obey. Then all will go well with you, and you will have many children in the land flowing with milk and honey, just as the LORD, the God of your ancestors, promised you.

⁴"Hear, O Israel! The LORD is our God, the LORD alone. ⁵And you must love the LORD your God with all your heart, all your soul, and all your strength. ⁶And you must commit yourselves wholeheartedly to these commands I am giving you today. ⁷Repeat them again and again to your children. Talk about them when you are at home and when you are away on a journey, when you are lying down and when you are getting up again. ⁸Tie them to your hands as a reminder, and wear them on your forehead. ⁹Write them on the doorposts of your house and on your gates."

INSIGHTS FOR LIFE

The word used for love *in these verses primarily speaks of an act of mind and will. It speaks of a committed, covenant love, not a love driven by transient, shallow emotion. Jesus spoke of this love when he quoted verse 5 to a lawyer who had asked him, "Teacher, which is the most important commandment in the law of Moses?" Speaking of this command from Deuteronomy, Jesus added, "This is the first and greatest commandment." If we love God with all of our heart, soul, and mind, the rest of God's commands will come naturally. Love for God is the basis for all obedience. Make a commitment today to truly love God—not with some temporary, halfhearted emotion, but with lasting, wholehearted devotion.*

Love Is the Greatest of All Spiritual Gifts

1 CORINTHIANS 13:1-13

¹If I could speak in any language in heaven or on earth but didn't love others, I would only be making meaningless noise

like a loud gong or a clanging cymbal. ²If I had the gift of prophecy, and if I knew all the mysteries of the future and knew everything about everything, but didn't love others, what good would I be? And if I had the gift of faith so that I could speak to a mountain and make it move, without love I would be no good to anybody. ³If I gave everything I have to the poor and even sacrificed my body, I could boast about it; but if I didn't love others, I would be of no value whatsoever.

⁴Love is patient and kind. Love is not jealous or boastful or proud ⁵or rude. Love does not demand its own way. Love is not irritable, and it keeps no record of when it has been wronged. ⁶It is never glad about injustice but rejoices whenever the truth wins out. ⁷Love never gives up, never loses faith, is always hopeful, and endures through every circumstance.

⁸Love will last forever, but prophecy and speaking in unknown languages and special knowledge will all disappear. ⁹Now we know only a little, and even the gift of prophecy reveals little! ¹⁰But when the end comes, these special gifts will all disappear.

¹¹It's like this: When I was a child, I spoke and thought and reasoned as a child does. But when I grew up, I put away childish things. ¹²Now we see things imperfectly as in a poor mirror, but then we will see everything with perfect clarity. All that I know now is partial and incomplete, but then I will know everything completely, just as God knows me now.

¹³There are three things that will endure—faith, hope, and love—and the greatest of these is love.

INSIGHTS FOR LIFE

This passage gives one of the most complete descriptions of love in the Bible. More important, it shows that love needs to be the one thing in life that we seek more than anything else. Without it, whatever we do or say really has no lasting value. Here God says that love is patient, kind, unselfish, and faithful. This is a far cry from the love we see in our world—a love that is impatient, rude, selfish, and temporary. The kind of love God wants us to give others is impossible to manufacture on our own. You might say that it is a "supernatural" love. It is the natural outflow of God's presence in our life. That is why the apostle Paul told the Roman believers, "[God] has given us the Holy Spirit to fill our hearts with his love."

Prayer

The Bible tells us, "Don't worry about anything; instead, pray about everything. Tell God what you need, and thank him for all he has done." For many, however, the idea of talking to God can be intimidating. But it doesn't have to be. In fact, prayer can be a wonderful experience if we know how to do it God's way. Fortunately, we have God's Word to teach us how to pray, and it tells us to pray at all times, in any posture, in any place, for any reason. It does not matter whether you pray in King James English or the most contemporary jargon. God only desires that you pray from a pure and sincere heart.

Why Should We Pray?

MATTHEW 26:36-44

³⁶Then Jesus brought them to an olive grove called Gethsemane, and he said, "Sit here while I go on ahead to pray." ³⁷He took Peter and Zebedee's two sons, James and John, and he began to be filled with anguish and deep distress. ³⁸He told them, "My soul is crushed with grief to the point of death. Stay here and watch with me."

³⁹He went on a little farther and fell face down on the ground, praying, "My Father! If it is possible, let this cup of

suffering be taken away from me. Yet I want your will, not mine." ⁴⁰Then he returned to the disciples and found them asleep. He said to Peter, "Couldn't you stay awake and watch with me even one hour? ⁴¹Keep alert and pray. Otherwise temptation will overpower you. For though the spirit is willing enough, the body is weak!"

⁴²Again he left them and prayed, "My Father! If this cup cannot be taken away until I drink it, your will be done." ⁴³He returned to them again and found them sleeping, for they just couldn't keep their eyes open.

⁴⁴So he went back to pray a third time, saying the same things again.

INSIGHTS FOR LIFE

The disciples observed the profound effect prayer had in Jesus' life and ministry. They witnessed how Jesus would often go off by himself to spend time in prayer with his heavenly Father. They saw the power, peace, and tranquillity that emanated from his life, giving him the ability to stay calm in troubled circumstances. Jesus' prayer life so impressed these men that they asked him to teach them to pray (the prayer he taught them is known as the Lord's Prayer). If the perfect Son of God often took time to pray during his life here on earth, how much more do we, mere men and women, need to pray?

How Should We Pray?

MATTHEW 6:5-13

⁵"And now about prayer. When you pray, don't be like the hypocrites who love to pray publicly on street corners and in the synagogues where everyone can see them. I assure you, that is all the reward they will ever get. ⁶But when you pray, go away by yourself, shut the door behind you, and pray to your Father secretly. Then your Father, who knows all secrets, will reward you.

⁷"When you pray, don't babble on and on as people of other

religions do. They think their prayers are answered only by repeating their words again and again. [8]Don't be like them, because your Father knows exactly what you need even before you ask him! [9]Pray like this:

Our Father in heaven,
    may your name be honored.
[10]May your Kingdom come soon.
May your will be done here on earth,
    just as it is in heaven.
[11]Give us our food for today,
[12]and forgive us our sins,
    just as we have forgiven those who have sinned
        against us.
[13]And don't let us yield to temptation,
    but deliver us from the evil one."

INSIGHTS FOR LIFE

When Jesus taught his disciples how to pray, he made it clear that they were not to show off, nor were they to babble on in an attempt to get God to respond to them. Instead, they were to present their requests simply and honestly, since God already knew their needs before they even asked. In Jesus' sample prayer, commonly called the Lord's Prayer, we see that he began by giving honor to God and praying for God's will to be done. Then he very directly asked God to meet our daily needs and to forgive our sins. Finally, he prays to be rescued from the evil one. While we do not need not use this exact prayer every time we pray, we should always pray with the same honesty and simplicity that this prayer displays.

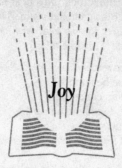

Joy

One noticeable change that takes place in a new believer's life is the inner joy he or she receives. In fact, joy is listed as a fruit of the Spirit that should be evident in every believer's life. But this joy is different from the fleeting and temporary *happiness* that is usually dependent upon good things happening in someone's life. While sorrows will certainly come our way, the Holy Spirit gives us inner joy and peace that cannot be taken away. Below are some of the ways we can experience God's joy in life.

Studying God's Word Helps Us Experience His Joy

NEHEMIAH 8:2-3, 5-6, 8-12

²So on October 8 Ezra the priest brought the scroll of the law before the assembly, which included the men and women and all the children old enough to understand. ³He faced the square just inside the Water Gate from early morning until noon and read aloud to everyone who could understand. All the people paid close attention to the Book of the Law.

⁵Ezra stood on the platform in full view of all the people. When they saw him open the book, they all rose to their feet.

⁶Then Ezra praised the LORD, the great God, and all the people chanted, "Amen! Amen!" as they lifted their hands toward heaven. Then they bowed down and worshiped the LORD with their faces to the ground.

⁸They read from the Book of the Law of God and clearly explained the meaning of what was being read, helping the people understand each passage. ⁹Then Nehemiah the governor, Ezra the priest and scribe, and the Levites who were interpreting for the people said to them, "Don't weep on such a day as this! For today is a sacred day before the LORD your God." All the people had been weeping as they listened to the words of the law.

¹⁰And Nehemiah continued, "Go and celebrate with a feast of choice foods and sweet drinks, and share gifts of food with people who have nothing prepared. This is a sacred day before our Lord. Don't be dejected and sad, for the joy of the LORD is your strength!"

¹¹And the Levites, too, quieted the people, telling them, "Hush! Don't weep! For this is a sacred day." ¹²So the people went away to eat and drink at a festive meal, to share gifts of food, and to celebrate with great joy because they had heard God's words and understood them.

INSIGHTS FOR LIFE

As we read this account, we see how the study of God's Word should lead to joy. Simply reading the Bible and studying its contents is not enough. Several other things must also take place. We must make the study of God's Word a priority. Our study of God's Word should lead to worship. We need to take time to understand what passages mean. We need to rejoice about what we have learned and share it with others. We need to apply what we have learned. As we study, understand, and obey God's Word, it produces joy in our life. And that joy of the Lord will be our strength, carrying us through the trials of life.

Knowing and Trusting God Brings Great Joy

1 PETER 1:3-9

³All honor to the God and Father of our Lord Jesus Christ, for it is by his boundless mercy that God has given us the privilege of being born again. Now we live with a wonderful expectation because Jesus Christ rose again from the dead. ⁴For God has reserved a priceless inheritance for his children. It is kept in heaven for you, pure and undefiled, beyond the reach of change and decay. ⁵And God, in his mighty power, will protect you until you receive this salvation, because you are trusting him. It will be revealed on the last day for all to see. ⁶So be truly glad! There is wonderful joy ahead, even though it is necessary for you to endure many trials for a while.

⁷These trials are only to test your faith, to show that it is strong and pure. It is being tested as fire tests and purifies gold—and your faith is far more precious to God than mere gold. So if your faith remains strong after being tried by fiery trials, it will bring you much praise and glory and honor on the day when Jesus Christ is revealed to the whole world.

⁸You love him even though you have never seen him. Though you do not see him, you trust him; and even now you are happy with a glorious, inexpressible joy. ⁹Your reward for trusting him will be the salvation of your souls.

INSIGHTS FOR LIFE

Many people today are seeking joy and happiness but not finding them. Perhaps people don't understand what true happiness is. At best, only fleeting happiness can be found in possessions, pleasures, or accomplishments. But the joy God gives is not just a feeling. It is not affected by our circumstances. In fact, it is an unchanging, natural by-product of our faith in Jesus Christ. As you trust in Jesus and look forward to his return, you will be filled with an "inexpressible joy." It won't be just some sort of emotional high. It will be a deep, supernatural experience of contentedness based upon the fact that your life is right with God. And this lasting joy and happiness will sustain you for the rest of your life.

Peace

Peace of mind—it seems elusive in a day when murders are commonplace, job security is nonexistent, and the moral fabric of society is falling apart. Yet Jesus has promised that each one of us can experience true peace: "I am leaving you with a gift—peace of mind and heart. And the peace I give isn't like the peace the world gives. So don't be troubled or afraid" (John 14:27). Unfortunately, some people are so caught up in the pursuit of peace, that they have forgotten that Jesus has already given it to them. They have simply left that gift "unopened." We cannot find peace outside of the parameters God has given us. As Augustine said many years ago, "Our souls are restless until they find their rest in God." Begin to "unwrap" this precious gift by examining what God's Word has to say about it.

Peace Begins When We Give Our Life to God
MATTHEW 11:25-30

²⁵Then Jesus prayed this prayer: "O Father, Lord of heaven and earth, thank you for hiding the truth from those who think themselves so wise and clever, and for revealing it to the childlike. ²⁶Yes, Father, it pleased you to do it this way!

²⁷"My Father has given me authority over everything. No

one really knows the Son except the Father, and no one really knows the Father except the Son and those to whom the Son chooses to reveal him."

²⁸Then Jesus said, "Come to me, all of you who are weary and carry heavy burdens, and I will give you rest. ²⁹Take my yoke upon you. Let me teach you, because I am humble and gentle, and you will find rest for your souls. ³⁰For my yoke fits perfectly, and the burden I give you is light."

INSIGHTS FOR LIFE

In this passage, Jesus teaches us three things we must do in order to find true peace or "rest." First, we need to come to Jesus. Those who have accepted Jesus Christ as Lord and Savior have already taken this step. Those who are still searching might be right at the door. But know this: True peace cannot be found in any other way. Second, we must exchange our yoke for his yoke. A yoke is a wooden harness placed across the shoulders of oxen so they can pull something. We need to remove the heavy yoke of sin and put on the lighter yoke of God's gracious forgiveness. Third, we need to let Jesus lead. This is hard because we want to be in control. But to find rest we must give God the reins so he can lead us.

We Need Christ's Peace to Rule in Our Heart

COLOSSIANS 3:12-17

¹²Since God chose you to be the holy people whom he loves, you must clothe yourselves with tenderhearted mercy, kindness, humility, gentleness, and patience. ¹³You must make allowance for each other's faults and forgive the person who offends you. Remember, the Lord forgave you, so you must forgive others. ¹⁴And the most important piece of clothing you must wear is love. Love is what binds us all together in perfect harmony. ¹⁵And let the peace that comes from Christ rule in your hearts. For as members of one body you are all called to live in peace. And always be thankful.

¹⁶Let the words of Christ, in all their richness, live in your

hearts and make you wise. Use his words to teach and counsel each other. Sing psalms and hymns and spiritual songs to God with thankful hearts. [17]And whatever you do or say, let it be as a representative of the Lord Jesus, all the while giving thanks through him to God the Father.

INSIGHTS FOR LIFE
One of the important marks of the Christian is peace. As Paul points out in verse 15, the peace of a Christian "comes from Christ" and "rules" in the heart. Christ's peace should act as an "umpire" or judge in our life, deciding our outlook no matter what the circumstances. What is Christ's peace like? As the apostle Paul told the Philippian church, it is not anxious about anything but trusts that God is in control. It doesn't forget God's blessings and answers to prayer. Christ's peace should be present in our relationships. It comes from Christ alone and is produced by the Holy Spirit. Christ's peace in us should promote peace with others. Give God your worries and concerns, and ask him to replace them with his peace.

Perseverance

There will be times in our Christian walk when we will feel emotionally down. We may think that God has forgotten about us. Or we might become discouraged as we see others who have believed in Jesus Christ lose interest and fall away. We may wonder whether we are next on the devil's "hit list." But God will not allow us to be hit with more than we can handle spiritually. In fact, it is during times of trouble that we will actually be strengthened, not weakened. As we read the Bible, we will come across words like *endurance* and *perseverance*. These words are often used when the Bible compares the Christian life to a race. The race referred to is a marathon, not a fifty-yard dash. Because the Christian life is a long-distance run, we need to pace ourselves, to persevere, and most of all, to *finish* the race.

Life's Trials Will Make Us Stronger
JAMES 1:2-18

²Dear brothers and sisters, whenever trouble comes your way, let it be an opportunity for joy. ³For when your faith is tested, your endurance has a chance to grow. ⁴So let it grow, for when your endurance is fully developed, you will be strong in character and ready for anything.

⁵If you need wisdom—if you want to know what God wants

you to do—ask him, and he will gladly tell you. He will not resent your asking. [6]But when you ask him, be sure that you really expect him to answer, for a doubtful mind is as unsettled as a wave of the sea that is driven and tossed by the wind. [7]People like that should not expect to receive anything from the Lord. [8]They can't make up their minds. They waver back and forth in everything they do.

[9]Christians who are poor should be glad, for God has honored them. [10]And those who are rich should be glad, for God has humbled them. They will fade away like a flower in the field. [11]The hot sun rises and dries up the grass; the flower withers, and its beauty fades away. So also, wealthy people will fade away with all of their achievements.

[12]God blesses the people who patiently endure testing. Afterward they will receive the crown of life that God has promised to those who love him. [13]And remember, no one who wants to do wrong should ever say, "God is tempting me." God is never tempted to do wrong, and he never tempts anyone else either. [14]Temptation comes from the lure of our own evil desires. [15]These evil desires lead to evil actions, and evil actions lead to death. [16]So don't be misled, my dear brothers and sisters.

[17]Whatever is good and perfect comes to us from God above, who created all heaven's lights. Unlike them, he never changes or casts shifting shadows. [18]In his goodness he chose to make us his own children by giving us his true word. And we, out of all creation, became his choice possession.

INSIGHTS FOR LIFE

One of the keys to growing and continuing to be effective in the Christian life is endurance. A key aspect of endurance is patience. This cheerful, enduring patience, which helps us to continue in our Christian walk, actually comes—and develops— in times of testing and hardship. During these "storms of life," our spiritual roots grow deeper, thus strengthening our faith. If we had our way, most of us would probably avoid these difficult times. Yet God promises that he will never give us more than we can handle. These times of trial and testing will either make us better or bitter. It really is up to us and the outlook we choose to take. We should view difficulties not as obstacles to our faith but as opportunities for spiritual growth.

Christ Endured Great Pain for Us

HEBREWS 12:1-13

¹Therefore, since we are surrounded by such a huge crowd of witnesses to the life of faith, let us strip off every weight that slows us down, especially the sin that so easily hinders our progress. And let us run with endurance the race that God has set before us. ²We do this by keeping our eyes on Jesus, on whom our faith depends from start to finish. He was willing to die a shameful death on the cross because of the joy he knew would be his afterward. Now he is seated in the place of highest honor beside God's throne in heaven. ³Think about all he endured when sinful people did such terrible things to him, so that you don't become weary and give up. ⁴After all, you have not yet given your lives in your struggle against sin.

⁵And have you entirely forgotten the encouraging words God spoke to you, his children? He said,

"My child, don't ignore it when the Lord disciplines you,
   and don't be discouraged when he corrects you.
⁶For the Lord disciplines those he loves,
   and he punishes those he accepts as his children."

⁷As you endure this divine discipline, remember that God is treating you as his own children. Whoever heard of a child who was never disciplined? ⁸If God doesn't discipline you as he does all of his children, it means that you are illegitimate and are not really his children after all. ⁹Since we respect our earthly fathers who disciplined us, should we

not all the more cheerfully submit to the discipline of our heavenly Father and live forever?

[10]For our earthly fathers disciplined us for a few years, doing the best they knew how. But God's discipline is always right and good for us because it means we will share in his holiness. [11]No discipline is enjoyable while it is happening—it is painful! But afterward there will be a quiet harvest of right living for those who are trained in this way.

[12]So take a new grip with your tired hands and stand firm on your shaky legs. [13]Mark out a straight path for your feet. Then those who follow you, though they are weak and lame, will not stumble and fall but will become strong.

INSIGHTS FOR LIFE

Jesus modeled the ultimate in endurance so that we would be encouraged to keep our faith strong in the race of life. Throughout the New Testament, the Christian life is compared to a race. With that in mind, we need to realize that it is not a short sprint but a long-distance run. Sometimes, as we are participating in this race, we can grow discouraged by circumstances or by what others say to us. But just as successful runners must keep their eyes on the prize, we, too, must remember what this race is all about. We must bear in mind for whom and to whom we are running: Jesus Christ. In essence, we need to keep our eyes on Jesus.

Purpose

It is a well-known fact that people are far more likely to enjoy something and do it well when they have a strong sense of purpose about it. This principle holds true even with life itself. The good news is that God has given us a great purpose for life: to be made like his Son, Jesus Christ. Along with this grand vision of our ultimate destiny, God has also given us purpose and direction for each day: to love him and to love our neighbors as ourselves. Such purpose should give us great joy and excitement about getting up each morning to start a new day, for we live for God and seek to follow his will for us. We can rest in the words of the prophet Jeremiah, "[God has] plans for good and not for disaster, to give you a future and a hope."

God Created Us to Do Good Things

EPHESIANS 2:1-10

¹Once you were dead, doomed forever because of your many sins. ²You used to live just like the rest of the world, full of sin, obeying Satan, the mighty prince of the power of the air. He is the spirit at work in the hearts of those who refuse to obey God. ³All of us used to live that way, following the passions and desires of our evil nature. We were born with an evil nature, and we were under God's anger just like everyone else.

⁴But God is so rich in mercy, and he loved us so very much, ⁵that even while we were dead because of our sins, he gave us life when he raised Christ from the dead. (It is only by God's special favor that you have been saved!) ⁶For he raised us from the dead along with Christ, and we are seated with him in the heavenly realms—all because we are one with Christ Jesus. ⁷And so God can always point to us as examples of the incredible wealth of his favor and kindness toward us, as shown in all he has done for us through Christ Jesus.

⁸God saved you by his special favor when you believed. And you can't take credit for this; it is a gift from God. ⁹Salvation is not a reward for the good things we have done, so none of us can boast about it. ¹⁰For we are God's masterpiece. He has created us anew in Christ Jesus, so that we can do the good things he planned for us long ago.

INSIGHTS FOR LIFE

God created us as good creatures, but we chose to turn away and enslave ourselves to sin. Fortunately the story does not end there. God, in his great mercy, chose to redeem us—that is, to buy us back from our slavery to sin and to free us to serve him once again. We are now free to fulfill the grand purpose for which God created us in the first place—to do good works for him. Each time we choose to obey God, each time we perform an act of love, each time we choose to do what is right we can take great joy in knowing that we are fulfilling God's great purpose for us. And all of this is because of God's grace toward us. We have not made ourselves good by our own efforts. God reached out to us even while we were sinful, and he has enabled us to do good things for him once again.

God Promises Us a Glorious Future

ROMANS 8:15-23

¹⁵So you should not be like cowering, fearful slaves. You should behave instead like God's very own children, adopted

into his family—calling him "Father, dear Father." [16]For his Holy Spirit speaks to us deep in our hearts and tells us that we are God's children. [17]And since we are his children, we will share his treasures—for everything God gives to his Son, Christ, is ours, too. But if we are to share his glory, we must also share his suffering.

[18]Yet what we suffer now is nothing compared to the glory he will give us later. [19]For all creation is waiting eagerly for that future day when God will reveal who his children really are. [20]Against its will, everything on earth was subjected to God's curse. [21]All creation anticipates the day when it will join God's children in glorious freedom from death and decay. [22]For we know that all creation has been groaning as in the pains of childbirth right up to the present time. [23]And even we Christians, although we have the Holy Spirit within us as a foretaste of future glory, also groan to be released from pain and suffering. We, too, wait anxiously for that day when God will give us our full rights as his children, including the new bodies he has promised us.

INSIGHTS FOR LIFE

Have you ever longed for something to happen? The Bible says that the whole world is longing for the day when it will be released from the curse of death and decay. This curse is a result of human disobedience, and it affects all creation. The good news of Jesus Christ is that there is hope that the curse will one day be broken. Even now, when we choose to follow Christ, he breaks the curse of sin within our hearts, releasing us from its power and freeing us to obey God. We still choose to sin from time to time, however. But the day is coming when Christ will release all creation from the curse of sin, and we will receive new bodies—ones that are no longer subject to sin and death. As the Bible tells us, let us not cower in the face of our struggles. Instead, let us live in the wonderful hope that those who belong to Christ are God's children, and they will be given great glory when he makes all things new once again.

The Bible

God can speak to people in many ways, but usually he simply uses the written message that he gave us long ago—the Bible. The apostle Paul once told a young church leader named Timothy just why the Bible is so important: "[The Scriptures] have given you the wisdom to receive the salvation that comes by trusting in Christ Jesus. All Scripture is inspired by God and is useful to teach us what is true and to make us realize what is wrong in our lives. It straightens us out and teaches us to do what is right. It is God's way of preparing us in every way, fully equipped for every good thing God wants us to do." All of these functions of the Bible that Paul mentioned are still true for us today.

The Bible Shows Us How to Live

PSALM 119:26-41

26I told you my plans, and you answered. Now teach me your principles. 27Help me understand the meaning of your commandments, and I will meditate on your wonderful miracles. 28I weep with grief; encourage me by your word. 29Keep me from lying to myself; give me the privilege of knowing your law. 30I have chosen to be faithful; I have determined to live by your laws. 31I cling to your decrees. LORD, don't let me be put to shame! ³²If you will help me, I will run to follow your commands.

³³Teach me, O LORD, to follow every one of your principles. ³⁴Give me understanding and I will obey your law; I will put it into practice with all my heart. ³⁵Make me walk along the path of your commands, for that is where my happiness is found. ³⁶Give me an eagerness for your decrees; do not inflict me with love for money! ³⁷Turn my eyes from worthless things, and give me life through your word. ³⁸Reassure me of your promise, which is for those who honor you. ³⁹Help me abandon my shameful ways; your laws are all I want in life. ⁴⁰I long to obey your commandments! Renew my life with your goodness.

⁴¹LORD, give to me your unfailing love, the salvation that you promised me.

INSIGHTS FOR LIFE
This section of Scripture is taken from a very long psalm that extols the virtues of God's Word. The psalmist desires to follow God's instructions for life and lists many blessings that flow out of them. These blessings still accompany obedience to God's Word today. By obeying God's Word, we will find that it encourages us. It keeps us from lying to ourselves. We will also find that God's Word brings us happiness. It turns our eyes from worthless things. It gives us life. God's Word reassures us of his promises. It also helps us abandon shameful ways. Finally God's Word shows us salvation. Let us rejoice in the many blessings that come from obeying God's Word!

The Bible Tells Us about Jesus
LUKE 24:13-34
¹³That same day two of Jesus' followers were walking to the village of Emmaus, seven miles out of Jerusalem. ¹⁴As they walked along they were talking about everything that had happened. ¹⁵Suddenly, Jesus himself came along and joined

them and began walking beside them. [16]But they didn't know who he was, because God kept them from recognizing him.

[17]"You seem to be in a deep discussion about something," he said. "What are you so concerned about?"

They stopped short, sadness written across their faces. [18]Then one of them, Cleopas, replied, "You must be the only person in Jerusalem who hasn't heard about all the things that have happened there the last few days."

[19]"What things?" Jesus asked.

"The things that happened to Jesus, the man from Nazareth," they said. "He was a prophet who did wonderful miracles. He was a mighty teacher, highly regarded by both God and all the people. [20]But our leading priests and other religious leaders arrested him and handed him over to be condemned to death, and they crucified him. [21]We had thought he was the Messiah who had come to rescue Israel. That all happened three days ago. [22]Then some women from our group of his followers were at his tomb early this morning, and they came back with an amazing report. [23]They said his body was missing, and they had seen angels who told them Jesus is alive! [24]Some of our men ran out to see, and sure enough, Jesus' body was gone, just as the women had said."

[25]Then Jesus said to them, "You are such foolish people! You find it so hard to believe all that the prophets wrote in the Scriptures. [26]Wasn't it clearly predicted by the prophets that the Messiah would have to suffer all these things before entering his time of glory?" [27]Then Jesus quoted passages from the writings of Moses and all the prophets, explaining what all the Scriptures said about himself.

[28]By this time they were nearing Emmaus and the end of their journey. Jesus would have gone on, [29]but they begged him to stay the night with them, since it was getting late. So he went home with them. [30]As they sat down to eat, he took a small loaf of bread, asked God's blessing on it, broke it, then

gave it to them. [31]Suddenly, their eyes were opened, and they recognized him. And at that moment he disappeared!

[32]They said to each other, "Didn't our hearts feel strangely warm as he talked with us on the road and explained the Scriptures to us?" [33]And within the hour they were on their way back to Jerusalem, where the eleven disciples and the other followers of Jesus were gathered. When they arrived, they were greeted with the report, [34]"The Lord has really risen! He appeared to Peter!"

INSIGHTS FOR LIFE

What is the greatest blessing of the Bible? The Scriptures tell us about the hope of humanity—Jesus Christ. From the first book of the Bible to the last, the Scriptures tell of the coming of God's Son into the world to save people from the plague of sin. Though they did not know who he was at the time, Jesus himself showed the two disciples these things as they traveled to Emmaus. What joy these disciples must have experienced when they realized that Jesus' death was not a sad end to a tragic story but rather a crucial part of God's plan of redemption. We can know that same joy as we come to believe that Jesus died for our sins and rose again in victory over death.

The Return
of Christ

With the turn of the millennium quickly approaching, interest in the end times is growing by leaps and bounds. Theories of every kind are being put forth regarding the end of the world. For many, all this talk of end times is very upsetting. For those who follow Christ, however, these questions should bring us only hope, for we know that whatever happens, Christ is coming back to take us to be with him in heaven. While we must be responsible to make the most of every opportunity to do good today, we need not worry ourselves over our ultimate destiny, for we are safe with Christ.

Christ Will Fulfill His Promise to Return

2 PETER 3:3-13

³First, I want to remind you that in the last days there will be scoffers who will laugh at the truth and do every evil thing they desire. ⁴This will be their argument: "Jesus promised to come back, did he? Then where is he? Why, as far back as anyone can remember, everything has remained exactly the same since the world was first created."

⁵They deliberately forget that God made the heavens by the word of his command, and he brought the earth up from

the water and surrounded it with water. ⁶Then he used the water to destroy the world with a mighty flood. ⁷And God has also commanded that the heavens and the earth will be consumed by fire on the day of judgment, when ungodly people will perish.

⁸But you must not forget, dear friends, that a day is like a thousand years to the Lord, and a thousand years is like a day. ⁹The Lord isn't really being slow about his promise to return, as some people think. No, he is being patient for your sake. He does not want anyone to perish, so he is giving more time for everyone to repent. ¹⁰But the day of the Lord will come as unexpectedly as a thief. Then the heavens will pass away with a terrible noise, and everything in them will disappear in fire, and the earth and everything on it will be exposed to judgment.

¹¹Since everything around us is going to melt away, what holy, godly lives you should be living! ¹²You should look forward to that day and hurry it along—the day when God will set the heavens on fire and the elements will melt away in the flames. ¹³But we are looking forward to the new heavens and new earth he has promised, a world where everyone is right with God.

INSIGHTS FOR LIFE

Just as the apostle Peter warned us, there are many today who are asking, "Why hasn't Christ returned yet? It's been two thousand years. Is he really coming back?" Many people demonstrate their disbelief in Christ's return by living as though there will be no consequences for their sin. Those who follow Christ, however, must remain faithful and trust that Christ is indeed coming back. We must also trust that God's timing is best. Peter tells us that God is waiting in order to give people more time to repent and receive his forgiveness. In other words, God is not being tardy by delaying Christ's return; he is being merciful. In the meantime, we must continue to obey what he has told us and look forward to that day when all will finally be made right.

Christ's Promise to Return Gives Us Hope

1 THESSALONIANS 4:13–5:2

13And now, brothers and sisters, I want you to know what will happen to the Christians who have died so you will not be full of sorrow like people who have no hope. 14For since we believe that Jesus died and was raised to life again, we also believe that when Jesus comes, God will bring back with Jesus all the Christians who have died.

15I can tell you this directly from the Lord: We who are still living when the Lord returns will not rise to meet him ahead of those who are in their graves. 16For the Lord himself will come down from heaven with a commanding shout, with the call of the archangel, and with the trumpet call of God. First, all the Christians who have died will rise from their graves. 17Then, together with them, we who are still alive and remain on the earth will be caught up in the clouds to meet the Lord in the air and remain with him forever. 18So comfort and encourage each other with these words.

5:1I really don't need to write to you about how and when all this will happen, dear brothers and sisters. 2For you know quite well that the day of the Lord will come unexpectedly, like a thief in the night.

INSIGHTS FOR LIFE

The death of a loved one is one of the greatest causes of sorrow that a person can experience. Yet, as the apostle Paul reminds us here, Christians need not be overcome with sorrow at the death of other Christians, for we know that one day we will see them again. A day is coming, Paul says, when Christ will appear in the sky along with all his followers who have died. When that happens, the followers of Christ who are still living will rise up and join them in the air. It will be a time of reunion and victory for all believers. While the passing of loved ones will always contain a certain amount of sadness, this great promise should fill believers with an undercurrent of hope even in the midst of sorrow.

How We Can Know God

What's Missing in Our Life?
"So I decided there is nothing better than to enjoy food and drink and to find satisfaction in work. Then I realized that this pleasure is from the hand of God. For who can eat or enjoy anything apart from him?" (Ecclesiastes 2:24-25) Purpose, meaning, a reason for living—these are all things we desire and search for in life. But despite our search, we still feel empty and unfulfilled. We each have an empty place in our heart, a spiritual void, a "God-shaped vacuum." Possessions won't fill it, nor will success, relationships, or even religion. Only through a vibrant relationship with God can this void be filled, but before such a relationship can be established, we need to face a serious problem.

The Problem: Sin
"The human heart is most deceitful and desperately wicked. Who really knows how bad it is?" (Jeremiah 17:9) The Bible identifies this problem as sin. Sin is not just the bad things we do but an inherent part of who we are. We are not sinners because we sin; we sin because we are sinners. King David once wrote, "I was born a sinner—yes, from the moment my

mother conceived me" (Psalm 51:5). Because we are born sinners, sinning comes to us naturally. And every problem we experience in society today can be traced back to our refusal to live God's way.

The Solution: Jesus Christ

"We are made right in God's sight when we trust in Jesus Christ to take away our sins. And we can all be saved in this same way, no matter who we are or what we have done." *(Romans 3:22)* God understood our problem and knew we could not beat it alone. So he lovingly sent his own Son, Jesus Christ, to bridge the chasm of sin that separates us from God. Jesus laid aside his divine privileges and walked the earth as a man, experiencing all the troubles and emotions that we do. Then he was arrested on false charges and killed on a Roman cross. But this was no accident. He did it to suffer the punishment deserved by us all. And then three days later, Jesus rose from the dead, conquering sin and death forever!

The Response: Accepting God's Offer

"Now turn from your sins and turn to God, so you can be cleansed of your sins." *(Acts 3:19)* To know Jesus Christ personally and have our sins forgiven, we must believe that we are sinners separated from God and that our only hope is Jesus Christ, the Son of God, who came and died for our sins. But we must not stop with this realization. We also need to take steps toward confessing and turning from our sins. And we must welcome Jesus Christ into our life as Lord and Savior. He will move in and help us to change from the inside out.

If you are ready to repent of your sins and believe in Jesus Christ so that you can receive his forgiveness, take a moment to pray like this:

God, I'm sorry for my sins. Right now, I turn from my sins and ask you to forgive me. Thank you for sending Jesus Christ to die on the cross for my sins. Jesus, I ask you to come into my life and be my Lord, Savior, and Friend. Thank you for forgiving me and giving me eternal life. In Jesus' name I pray. Amen.

If you prayed this prayer and meant it, you can be sure that God has forgiven you and received you into his family.

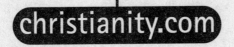

Site opens June 1, 2000

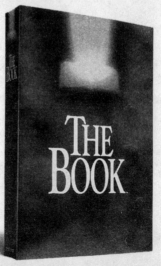

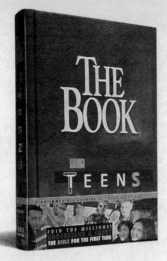
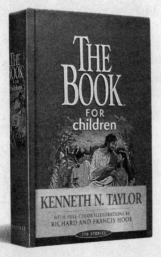